D1810278

City of Westminster

Contents

What is an engineer?

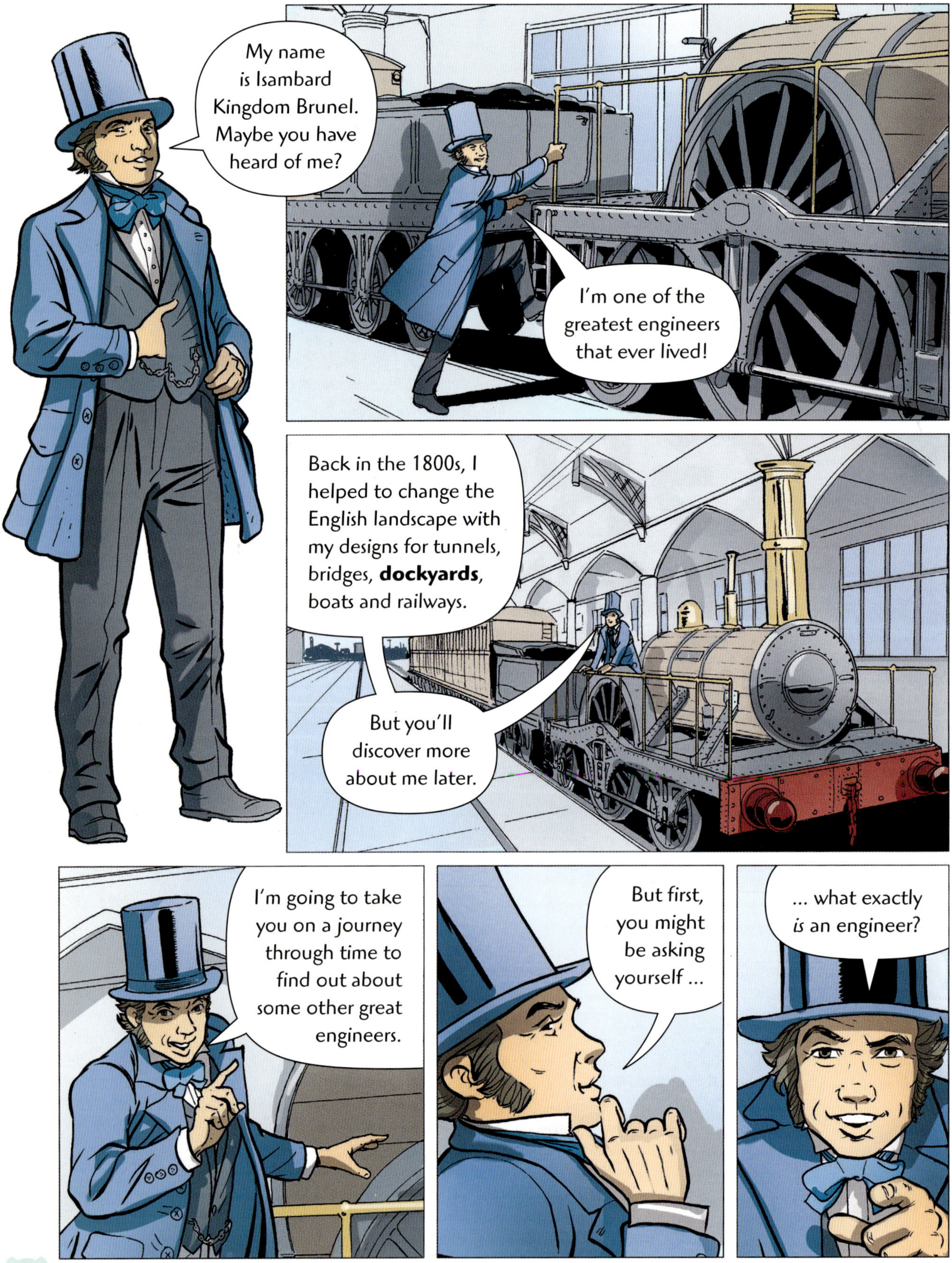

My name is Isambard Kingdom Brunel. Maybe you have heard of me?

I'm one of the greatest engineers that ever lived!

Back in the 1800s, I helped to change the English landscape with my designs for tunnels, bridges, **dockyards**, boats and railways.

But you'll discover more about me later.

I'm going to take you on a journey through time to find out about some other great engineers.

But first, you might be asking yourself …

… what exactly *is* an engineer?

Engineers are people who design and construct things to improve our lives. Without them, the world would be very different.

Without engineers, there would be no planes, helicopters or spacecraft.

There would be no bridges or skyscrapers.

There would be no bicycles, cars or trains ...

... no mobile phones or computers (or coffee machines!) ...

... and no X-ray machines or life-support systems.

EVERY machine, building, appliance and device has been engineered.

There have been engineers since the start of human history.

Throughout the centuries, their work has changed our world. Let's meet some of them.

Imhotep

First, let's meet an engineer who lived over four thousand years ago.

Egypt, around 2650 BC ...

Ancient Egypt is famous for its massive stone pyramids.

However, the first Egyptian buildings were made of mud bricks, not stone.

Your palace is nearly finished, my king.

Hmmm ...

Djoser was a king of Egypt who wanted something new ...

This won't last for long!

Djoser decided he wanted his tomb made entirely from stone.

I want my buildings to last forever. Summon Imhotep!

Imhotep is known as history's first engineer.

He designed all of Djoser's buildings.

However, building in stone was a new challenge.

TAP
TAP
TAP

It will mean dragging huge blocks of stone for several miles ...

... and making them all fit together.

Tricky ... but not impossible.

Imhotep didn't realize it then, but he was about to design the largest stone building in the world!

Imhotep drew up plans for the king's tomb.

The stone building will be on top, but the king will be buried deep underground ...

... in a **sarcophagus** the size of a small room.

There will be many underground rooms and tunnels ...

... filled with precious objects.

Egyptian kings required grand burial chambers, to demonstrate their power and wealth even in death.

Imhotep put his men to work.

How much deeper do we dig?

28 metres!

It took many months to complete Djoser's tomb.

But the king was not impressed.

Your tomb, Majesty.

Imhotep, this is too flat! Make me a building that reaches to the stars!

Imhotep had no option but to accept the challenge.

I could build another **mastaba** on top ... or maybe several?

I could make the biggest building in the world!

Imhotep assembled a massive workforce which was split into two teams.

You lot, come with me.

Huge sledges were used to drag limestone blocks up ramps and into place.

Ready ... and PULL!

Simple tools were used to finish the stone blocks.

A little more off the corner.

This time the building work took many years, not months, to complete.

But at last it was finished.

It is done, Majesty.

Wow!

Djoser's funeral complex had buildings, courtyards, temples and tombs for the king and his whole family.

The greatest building of all was the sixty-metre-high Step Pyramid. It was the largest stone structure built in its time.

60m

Beneath the pyramid, your tomb has over four hundred rooms.

It is superb! Imhotep, you are a genius.

- Imhotep was the first recorded engineer in history.
- He was also Egypt's first recorded doctor. He knew how to stop wounds from becoming infected.
- Imhotep was the 'patron of scribes'. Egyptian scribes (writers) were important people in Ancient Egypt and it took many years of training to become one.
- Imhotep's Step Pyramid still stands today and is considered an amazing feat of engineering even by modern standards.
- The Step Pyramid was the first of several Ancient Egyptian pyramids. It took eighteen years to complete, which was nearly as long as King Djoser's entire reign.
- In later years, pyramids went out of fashion and pharaohs were instead buried in underground tombs in the Valley of the Kings in Egypt.

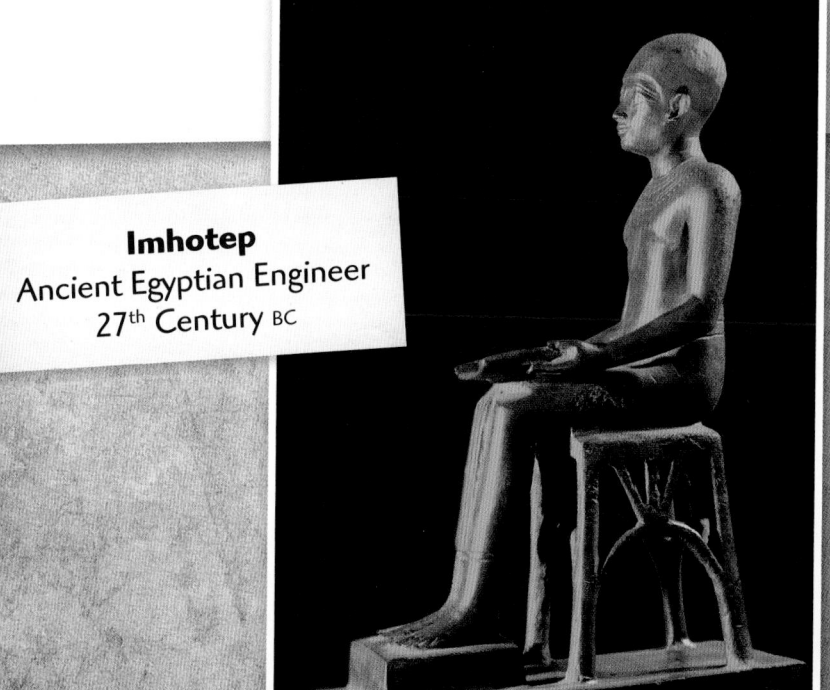

Imhotep
Ancient Egyptian Engineer
27th Century BC

Apollodorus of Damascus

We need to go to Ancient Rome to meet our next engineer.

Roman Empire, around 100 AD ...

The Romans were great engineers. They built large, arched bridges, **amphitheatres**, public baths, **aqueducts**, and roads that connected the Roman Empire.

The Roman Army travelled along its roads to conquer new territories.

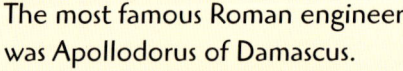

Quick march, quick march!

The army built new Roman towns wherever it went. For this reason, engineers always travelled with them.

The most famous Roman engineer was Apollodorus of Damascus.

Apollodorus was a clever engineer. He designed many war machines for the army.

Emperor Trajan loved Apollodorus's machines.

What have you brought me today, Apollodorus?

A tower with ladders for climbing over enemy walls ...

... a wooden 'tortoise' for protecting soldiers ...

... and battering rams for smashing down enemy gates.

Trajan asked Apollodorus to join him in war, battling Rome's enemies.

We need you to build a bridge across the Danube River.

Apollodorus rode with Trajan's army.

There it is, Apollodorus: the Danube.

It's so wide! This will be the greatest engineering challenge of my life.

I'll need to build twenty large stone pillars across the river.

Then I'll attach wooden arches between the pillars.

We will need boats to put the pillars in place.

On Apollodorus's advice, boats were tied together across the river.

This is called a pontoon bridge.

The pillars were driven into the river bed ...

... and built forty-five metres high.

It was dangerous work.

Help! Help!

Hurry up, Trajan is impatient.

Trajan's Bridge was finished in 105 AD. It was 1135 metres long.

Your bridge is a triumph, Apollodorus.

Thank you, Emperor.

Back in Rome, Apollodorus designed many of the city's buildings ...

Apollodorus built this **forum**.

... structures that are still admired today!

His most famous work is Trajan's Column.

It's so tall!

Wow!

Only a great engineer could design a column like this!

Trajan's Column is thirty metres high with intricate **friezes** extending the whole way up.

The friezes on Trajan's column taught the modern world about Ancient Roman engineering techniques, including the construction of Trajan's Bridge.

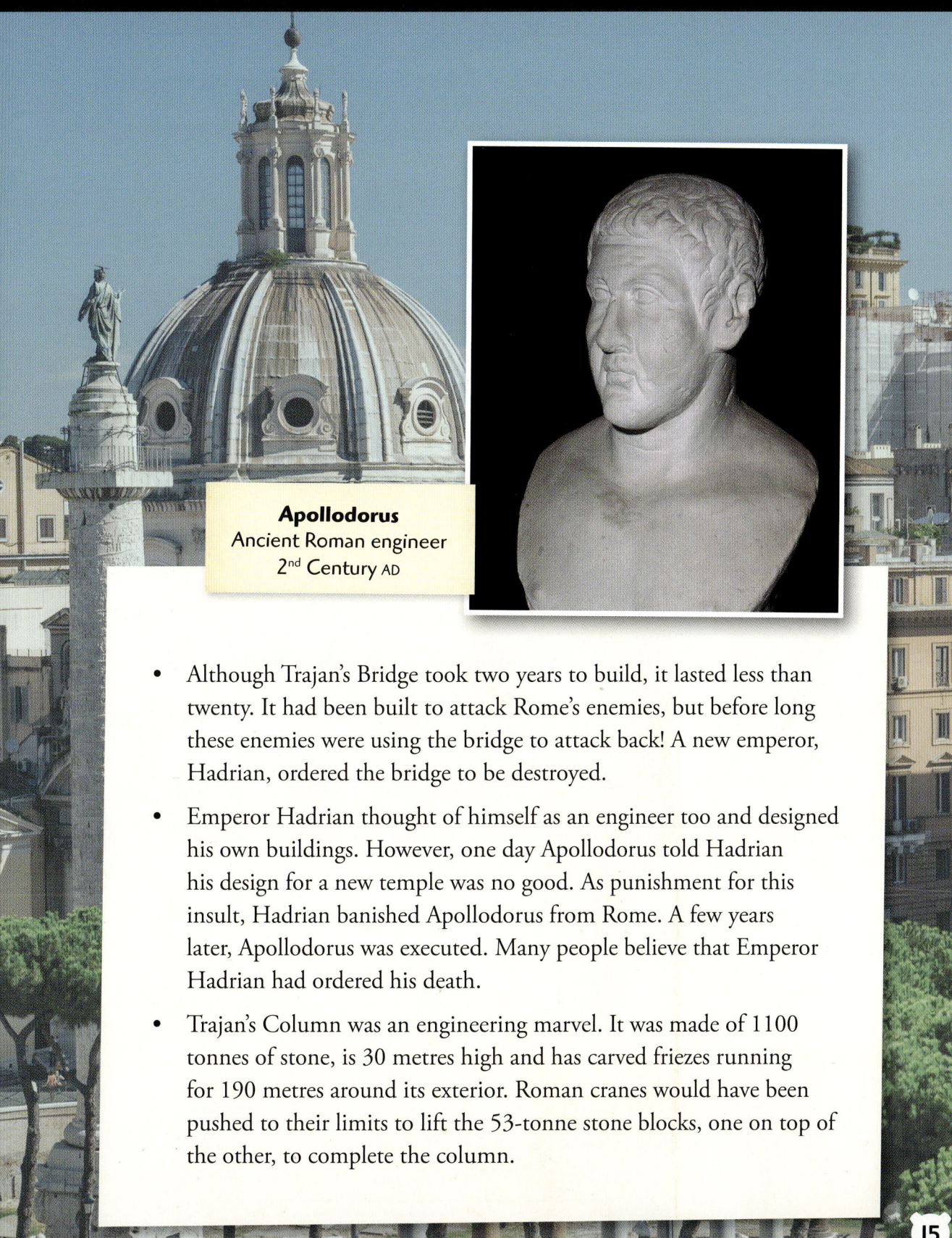

Apollodorus
Ancient Roman engineer
2nd Century AD

- Although Trajan's Bridge took two years to build, it lasted less than twenty. It had been built to attack Rome's enemies, but before long these enemies were using the bridge to attack back! A new emperor, Hadrian, ordered the bridge to be destroyed.

- Emperor Hadrian thought of himself as an engineer too and designed his own buildings. However, one day Apollodorus told Hadrian his design for a new temple was no good. As punishment for this insult, Hadrian banished Apollodorus from Rome. A few years later, Apollodorus was executed. Many people believe that Emperor Hadrian had ordered his death.

- Trajan's Column was an engineering marvel. It was made of 1100 tonnes of stone, is 30 metres high and has carved friezes running for 190 metres around its exterior. Roman cranes would have been pushed to their limits to lift the 53-tonne stone blocks, one on top of the other, to complete the column.

Isambard Kingdom Brunel

Hello again. This part of the book is all about – you guessed it – me!

I was born in 1806, but we're picking up my story when I was a young man.

London 1826: Isambard began his first engineering project at just nineteen years old.

At the time, Isambard's father, Marc, was designing the Thames Tunnel: a 396 metre-long tunnel underneath the River Thames in London.

People flocked to see the tunnel under construction.

Step up ... one shilling for a look inside the tunnel!

Will it be waterproof?

Finishing the tunnel made Isambard's father sick with worry.

I can't cope! Isambard, you'll have to take over.

Isambard loved the challenge of his first engineering project.

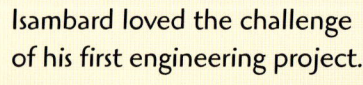

Thanks for coming!

During construction, Isambard even held a dinner in the tunnel to demonstrate that it was safe.

The Thames Tunnel was the first underwater tunnel anywhere in the world. It was one of the most ambitious engineering projects of its time ...

... and Isambard worked tirelessly to finish it.

However, it was a dangerous project.

The river's coming in!

Evacuate!

Help!

Hurry!

Isambard's assistant dragged him to safety just in time. Six men lost their lives in the flood.

Are you all right, sir?

Isambard's doctor sent him to Bristol to recover.

Work on the tunnel stopped for several years, but it was eventually opened in 1843.

In 1829, while in Bristol, Isambard saw a competition in a paper ...

A bridge across the Avon Gorge! *I* could design a bridge.

I could build towers on either side of the river to suspend the bridge.

1352m

75m

At first, Isambard didn't win the competition ...

The Gorge is too wide for a suspension bridge!

I disagree. People have been building suspension bridges across large distances for hundreds of years!

No one won the competition, so a second competition was launched. This time Isambard managed to convince the panel to give him first prize.

My bridge will be stronger, last longer and cost less to build than all the other entries!

Building the bridge was fraught with danger.

That's a 100 metre drop to the bottom!

Materials were sent across the deep gorge in a basket which travelled along a 1000 metre iron bar.

I'll prove this basket is safe!

It's too dangerous, boss!

Isambard was more than just a great engineer. He was also a great leader.

He's stuck!

The basket became snagged halfway across ...

... and Isambard had to free it by climbing out and fixing the snag.

I can't watch!

It was another brush with danger for Isambard, who earned a reputation for being a **daredevil**.

Hooray for the boss!

In 1832, the only way to get from London to the west of England was by horse.

Yet everywhere else in the country railways were springing up.

Isambard, we want you to build a railway between London and Bristol.

Isambard did some **research**. He thought other railways were too bumpy.

I can't even hold my hand steady.

My railway has got to be as flat, fast and smooth as a **billiard** table.

To ensure that his railway track stayed flat, Isambard constructed amazing **viaducts** and bridges.

Isambard worked hard. Sometimes he even helped with the digging.

There were many obstacles to building the railway ...

What about these hills, boss?

We'll have to tunnel through.

Impossible! You'd have to build the world's longest tunnel to get through Box Hill.

Nothing's impossible!

No one believed Isambard could build the Box Hill Tunnel.

It's solid rock – you'll never get through it.

The roof will cave in.

It will be hard work, but we can do it!

Isambard began building the tunnel anyway.

Come on, lads. You can do it!

About 4000 workers had to **excavate** the tunnel with shovels ...

... and gunpowder.

BOOM

Look out!

Over 300 horses carted out the rock.

One tonne of candles and one tonne of gunpowder were used every week.

Sir, sir, we've broken through!

After five years the Box Hill Tunnel was eventually finished.

Isambard finally completed his Great Western Railway.

Queen Victoria herself travelled on the line.

It took four hours to get from London to Bristol, instead of thirteen hours by horse.

Well done, Brunel!

Isambard had proved he was a great engineer who could turn his hand to anything. However, nobody guessed what was coming next.

Hmm, I think I need a new challenge.

Isambard went from steam trains to building steamships!

He built the *Great Western* ...

Then he built the *Great Britain* ...

... and then the *Great Eastern*.

The *Great Eastern* will be six times larger than the world's biggest ship!

She will carry 4000 passengers plus cargo.

Sadly, Isambard did not live to see its **maiden voyage**.

The *Great Eastern* finally set sail a few weeks after Isambard's death. She was the largest ship the world had ever seen and made many voyages across the Atlantic.

- Isambard is known for his many engineering 'firsts'. He built the first tunnel under a river and developed the first iron ship powered by a propeller.

- Some of Isambard's other famous engineering accomplishments include Paddington Station and the Royal Albert Bridge, both in London.

- Isambard also designed many of Britain's major docks, including those in Bristol and Cardiff.

- The Thames Tunnel opened in 1843, the same year the *Great Britain* first sailed. Today it is used as part of the London railway network.

- Isambard died on 15th September 1859, aged 53, following news of an explosion on board the *Great Eastern* during her sea trials.

- Isambard's Clifton Suspension Bridge was never finished in his lifetime. It was finally completed in 1864.

- Isambard Kingdom Brunel is today remembered as Britain's greatest engineer. He was known as a workaholic who would never give up. Isambard proved he could overcome any obstacle to realize his dreams.

Isambard Kingdom Brunel
Victorian Engineer
9th April 1806–
15th September 1859

Emily Roebling

Brooklyn, New York, 1872 ...

We have to go to America to meet our next great engineer ...

Emily Roebling was one of three chief engineers who built the Brooklyn Bridge.

She had no engineering qualifications or experience. Instead, she had to learn on the job.

Emily's father-in-law, John Roebling, originally designed the bridge.

Later, Emily's husband, Washington, took over as chief engineer.

First, we sink a wooden box called a '**caisson**', dig down into the river bed from there and fill the hole with concrete.

Washington had to build the bridge's towers.

But working in the caisson was dangerous.

Are you all right, boss?

In January 1872, Emily received bad news.

It's your husband ...

Is he all right?

He just collapsed!

He'll live, but he has **the bends** ...

... He'll be housebound from now on.

But he's the chief engineer! Who will finish the bridge?

I will!

I've learned so much about engineering from you.

I'll teach you the rest!

Let's get these towers finished!

Yes, boss.

Emily studied hard: the strength of materials and the quantity of supplies all had to be worked out.

Washington helped from his sick room.

It's time to attach the cables.

We will need 488 metres of steel cable to be strung between the two towers.

Emily had to make sure everyone was doing their job.

This steel cable is not good enough!

Building the bridge was dangerous and difficult ...

... but Emily met every challenge.

The bridge will soon be finished.

Who is that?

It's the chief engineer, isn't it?

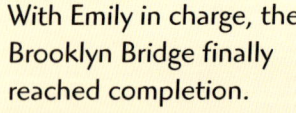

With Emily in charge, the Brooklyn Bridge finally reached completion.

On 24th May 1883, President Chester Arthur opened the bridge.

Politicians praised Emily.

To Emily Roebling!

Washington held a banquet in his room.

I thought I would **succumb** but I had a strong tower to lean on – my wife.

- It took twenty years for the Brooklyn Bridge to be built. It claimed the lives of twenty men, including John Roebling, its designer.

- Today, the Brooklyn Bridge is considered one of the great engineering feats of the modern age.

- Congressman Abram Hewitt said the bridge was: 'an everlasting monument to the self-sacrificing devotion of a woman and of her capacity for that higher education from which she has been too long disbarred.'

Emily Roebling
Chief engineer of the Brooklyn Bridge
23rd September 1843–
28th February 1903

- After the Brooklyn Bridge was finished, Emily Roebling designed a mansion in New Jersey for her and Washington to live in.

- Emily never received an official engineering qualification, but later earned a degree in law.

- Washington Roebling recovered from his illness some years after the Brooklyn Bridge was finished.

- Emily and Washington later travelled widely and met Tsar Nicholas II of Russia and Queen Victoria.

- Emily died in 1903. Washington lived until 1926.

Karl Benz

Karl Benz was one of the greatest mechanical engineers of all time.

Karl's mother had little money when he was a child.

There's not much tonight, Karl.

Karl helped his mother by fixing watches and clocks.

At seventeen, Karl studied engineering.

The steam train engine is too big and bulky ...

... something smaller needs to replace it!

What if I could build a smaller engine to transport people around, that ran on something other than steam?

I could call it the Horseless Carriage!

Later, Karl found work as an engineer; he had to work on his engine idea in his own time.

Karl met and married a young woman called Bertha.

My engine will run on petrol!

What a brilliant idea!

Karl quit his job and opened his own workshop.

In 1883, Karl went into business with bicycle shop owners Max Rose and Friedrich Esslinger.

BENZ & Co

In 1886, his automobile was finally ready ... though he had changed its name from the Horseless Carriage by then.

I call it the Motorwagen.

Karl and Bertha began testing the Motorwagen around their neighbourhood.

Yet not everyone liked the Motorwagen.

You're scaring the horses!

I thought people would love my Motorwagen, but they hate it.

More people need to see it, Karl.

One day, Bertha and her two sons took the Motorwagen ...

Ssshh, don't wake your father.

... and drove it on a 66-mile trip.

Now everybody will see the Motorwagen in action!

Bertha had to make repairs along the way.

The fuel line is blocked, Mum.

Let's use this hat pin.

She discovered many things about the Motorwagen.

It only goes up steep hills in reverse!

What is that?

After Bertha's trip, the orders piled in.

Bertha?

I want a Motorwagen!

Where do I buy one?

We've become the world's number one car manufacturer! I couldn't have done it without you, Bertha.

Karl Benz
Automotive engineer
25th November 1844–
4th April 1929

- Today Karl Benz is remembered as the engineer who invented the world's first petrol-powered automobile.

- Karl Benz's three-wheeled Motorwagen became the first ever car to be sold to the public.

- To start with, the Motorwagen only had two gears – forward and reverse. Bertha found that reverse was more powerful and drove up steep hills backwards. When she returned, she told Karl the Motorwagen needed another more powerful forward gear.

- Karl Benz built his first four-wheeled car, the Viktoria, in 1891.

- A later car, the Velo became the first car to be produced on a mass scale.

- By 1900, Benz & Co had become the world's leading automobile manufacturer.

- In 1903, Karl Benz retired from Benz & Co and the company then joined with its competitor, Daimler. Today the company is called Mercedes-Benz, and it continues to make cars.

- Karl Benz died in 1929 and Bertha in 1944.

Sergei Korolev

12th April, 1961 was a big day in the history of engineering.

A Soviet Union rocket was about to blast the first man into space.

Forward!

The rocket had been designed by engineer Sergei Korolev.

Vostok 1: at last!

Flying the rocket was **cosmonaut** Yuri Gagarin.

Are you ready, Yuri?

Ready!

At approximately 7am, everything was ready.

All systems are go.

Five ... four ... three ... two ... one ... lift-off!

When he was young, Sergei loved two things: mathematics and planes.

Yes, Sergei?

$12 \times \frac{3}{4} =$

As a teenager, Sergei built his own glider.

Your glider flies, Sergei!

After studying at university, Sergei designed planes which were powered by rockets.

Later, Sergei became the chief engineer of the Soviet Union space programme.

I have designed the most powerful rocket in the world. It can reach space.

We will use this R-7 rocket to blast our satellite, called Sputnik, into space.

Then it will fly around the world for everyone to see.

WARP WARP

The launch of Sputnik caused a great stir.

The Soviet Union has sent a satellite into space.

We Americans need to send something into space too!

A space race began between the Soviet Union and the USA.

The Americans are sending a satellite into space.

That's nothing. We are sending a dog into space!

The Russians didn't just want to send dogs into space ... they wanted to send people.

One of you will be chosen to travel into space aboard *Vostok 1*.

The first man in space. What an honour!

The launch of *Vostok 1* amazed the world. The capsule carrying Yuri Gagarin flew around the globe ...

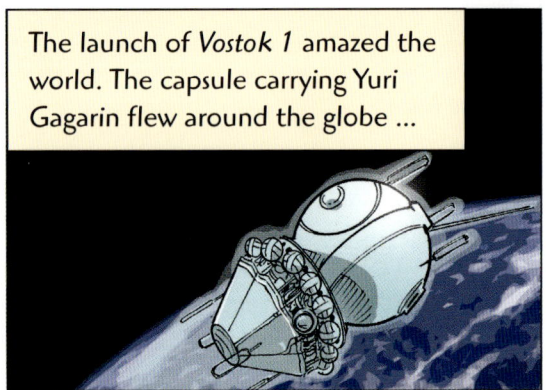

... and landed back on Earth in a field.

Yuri Gagarin became the most famous man on Earth.

However, no-one knew about Sergei Korolev ...

... the engineer who had sent a man into space!

- As the Soviet Union's chief space designer, Sergei Korolev was kept hidden from the world. However, he is considered one of the greatest aeronautical engineers of all time. Most people only learned about Sergei when he died in 1966.

- Sergei developed his R-7 rocket from the V2 rocket the Nazis built in World War II to destroy cities. At that time, the V2 could fly further than any other rocket.

- Sergei realized he could use the V2 technology to develop a rocket that could reach space. At the time, nobody believed that this was possible.

- Just before he died, Sergei was designing a space rocket to send men to the Moon. Instead, America sent the first man to the Moon in 1969, winning the space race.

- The space race meant engineers made many new breakthroughs in technology. This space technology has since been used for many things on Earth that today we take for granted. These include everything from reflective food wrappers to micro-parts used to create artificial limbs.

Sergei Korolev
Aeronautical engineer
12th January 1907 –
14th January 1966

More great engineers

Here are some other great engineers you may not have heard of ...

Alexandre-Gustave Eiffel was a French civil engineer who constructed the Eiffel Tower in Paris. He was also the chief engineer on the Statue of Liberty in New York.

Nikola Tesla was an electrical and a mechanical engineer. He is best known for his work on **alternating current** and the electricity supply system.

The Wright brothers were American inventors and engineers who are widely credited with building the world's first aeroplane.

Everyone calls me Elsie or 'Queen of the Hurricanes'.

Elsie MacGill was the world's first female aircraft designer. During WWII she helped to build the Hawker Hurricane aircraft used by the Royal Air Force (RAF).

Fazul Rahman Khan was a structural engineer who paved the way for high-rise building design in the 20th century.

I designed the famous Willis Tower, in Chicago.

Judith Resnik was an electrical engineer for NASA and the second ever American female astronaut.

I had the idea for the hand-held mobile phone.

Martin or 'Marty' Cooper is an American engineer in the communications industry. He made the first ever mobile phone call in 1973.

James Dyson is a British inventor and design engineer. He makes low-energy, eco-friendly products, like the famous bagless vacuum cleaner.

Aprille Ericsson-Jackson is a mechanical engineer. She was the first African-American woman to receive a PhD in Engineering at the NASA Goddard Space Flight Center.

Now you know how great engineers can be ... do you think you'd like to be one?

Glossary

alternating current	an electrical current where the direction changes frequently
amphitheatre	a public arena in Ancient Rome
aqueduct	a channel for transporting water
bends, the	sickness, experienced sometimes when a person's body experiences extreme pressure, most frequently when in very deep water
billiards	a game for two people in which three balls are struck with cues into pockets around the edge of a table
caisson	a large watertight container which is used to carry out construction work under water. It is open at the bottom and the water is kept out by air pressure.
cosmonaut	a Russian space explorer
dockyard	an area with docks and equipment for repairing and maintaining ships
daredevil	a reckless person who enjoys dangerous things
excavate	make a hole or channel by digging
frieze	a painted or sculptured band of decoration
forum	a public square or marketplace used for judicial and other business in Ancient Rome
maiden voyage	the first voyage undertaken by a ship
mastaba	an Ancient Egyptian flat-topped tomb
research	the investigation into and study of materials and sources in order to establish facts and reach new conclusions
sarcophagus	a tomb or coffin in Ancient Egypt
succumb	failure to resist pressure or some other negative force
viaduct	a raised structure consisting of a series of arches to carry a road or railway

Index